REFLECTIONS

OF A

VIETNAM VET

By

R. Jack Santos

Order this book online at www.trafford.com/09-0401
or email orders@trafford.com

Most Trafford titles are also available at major online book retailers.

Note for Librarians: A cataloguing record for this book is available from Library
and Archives Canada at www.collectionscanada.ca/amicus/index-e.html

Printed in Victoria, BC, Canada.

ISBN: 978-1-4251-6574-1(sc)

ISBN: 978-1-4269-0142-3 (e-book)

*We at Trafford believe that it is the responsibility of us all, as both individuals
and corporations, to make choices that are environmentally and socially sound.
You, in turn, are supporting this responsible conduct each time you purchase a
Trafford book, or make use of our publishing services. To find out how you are
helping, please visit www.trafford.com/responsiblepublishing.html*

*Our mission is to efficiently provide the world's finest, most comprehensive
book publishing service, enabling every author to experience success.
To find out how to publish your book, your way, and have it available
worldwide, visit us online at www.trafford.com*

 www.trafford.com

North America & international
toll-free: 1 888 232 4444 (USA & Canada)
phone: 250 383 6864 ♦ fax: 250 383 6804 ♦ email: info@trafford.com

The United Kingdom & Europe
phone: +44 (0)1865 487 395 ♦ local rate: 0845 230 9601
facsimile: +44 (0)1865 481 507 ♦ email: info.uk@trafford.com

10 9 8 7 6 5 4 3 2 1

DEDICATION

This book is dedicated to my father, Cornelio Santos. I hope I was able to make him proud of me. He understood that going to Vietnam was something I had to do. My mother, Cora Duran, I never really got to know her but now I wish I had. My brother, Tom Santos who surprised me once when he told me he was proud of me as I was doing something he didn't think he could. My Grandparents, John and Maria Santos, I miss you all but you have gone to a better place. One day, we will be reunited.

This book is also dedicated to (El Tee) Gerald Palma who was my platoon leader with the 17th Cav in 1966. He returned to Vietnam on a second tour as a Captain of Infantry and was killed in action. It is also dedicated to Sgt. (Andy) Andujar, Wayne Garrett and DJ, a nickname as I can't recall his real name but he was a good bro. To the rest of those that lost their lives and are now enshrined on the Vietnam War Memorial.

Author Bio

I had two enlistments in the U.S. Army, 1966-1967 and 1968-1971. In the six years, I served three tours in Vietnam as a medic with the Infantry. 1966 was with the 2nd Squadron, 17th Cavalry, 1st Brigade of the 101st Airborne Division. 1968-1969 with the 4th Battalion, 12th Infantry of the 199th Light Infantry Brigade and 1970-1971 with the 4th Battalion 503rd Infantry, 173rd Airborne Brigade. I departed with the 173rd Airborne Brigade when it was withdrawn from Vietnam and ended my service at Fort Campbell, Ky.

I was awarded the following medals while in service: Parachute Wings, Combat Medic Badge, two Purple Hearts, two Bronze Stars, three Army Commendation Medals, Vietnam Campaign Medal with five campaign stars and the National Defense Service Medal.

After twenty nine years in law enforcement I retired and live in Colorado.

CONTENTS

REFLECTIONS OF A VIETNAM VET

CONTENTS

Journey To War

When I was a young and restless kid
I surprised my family by what I did
I joined the Army – Airborne Infantry
Figured the training would be good for me

A Paratrooper, I wanted to be
Could I survive the training, I had to see
Three weeks of Airborne training hell
When I received my wings, my chest did swell

At Fort Campbell, a Major asked some to change their specialty
I became a medic, called "Doc" by the Infantry
In 1965, 1st Brigade, 101st Airborne Division was sent to Vietnam
The Screaming Eagles would fight again, do the VC harm

I volunteered and received my orders at end of year
Soon, too soon, combat would show me a new type of fear
In battle after battle, we fought VC, we fought NVA
For our bros, no price too big to pay

Politicians were to blame for a war that was lost
They paid no attention to us, we who paid the cost
Am I bitter, they didn't let us win? Sure I am
But I'm still proud to say, "I went to Vietnam"

G I Blues

My country called, I went to war
A young boy far from home
We called it "Nam". War made it hell
We killed and died in a strange far land
We'd sweep a village and lose a few
We'd walk the rice paddies and lose there too
The Viet Cong lost men too
If more died then could flee
The Brass would call it a victory

Back in camp, we'd mourn our dead
Shed a tear, no more said
By dark of night, we'd sneak around
To ambush Charlie, he must be found
The ambush works, VC in flight
Machine guns roar, flares light the night
It's calm in seconds, no one moves
"Medic" is softly cried
I hold a boy, an American G I
Eighteen….too young to die
I look to Heaven and ask God…why

We fought, we died, no one cared
The rich, the famous, fled our land
Left the poor, the loyal, to fight our stand
I helped a friend with one last smoke
He gave a sigh and then was gone
I cried…not for him…not for me
Politicians refused to see

We couldn't win, too many rules to tie us down
We fought pitch battles, day and night
America's youth, America's might

In a year, the Freedom Bird
Home at last, no scars to show
The nightmares start, the dreams do too
Why did I live? I'd like to know
The guilt is heavy....too heavy at times
Among nations, America stands tall
For her youth gave their all

NOMADS OF VIETNAM

The 101st Airborne was sent to Vietnam
VC mothers tell your sons goodbye
When we meet, they will die
Grab your tissue, prepare to cry

Cheo Rio, Tuy Hoa, Dak To
VC run but don't run too slow
Look behind you, see the Eagle patch
Pray to Buddha, your life we don't snatch

We are Airborne, we are proud
The Eagle scream will be long and loud
We are lean, we are mean
We are one badass fighting machine

Stay alert, stay alive
That's our motto, we don't jive
So run VC run, we're just no fun
You'll meet your death from the One-O-One

2/17ᵀᴴ CAV

I was sent to Vietnam to the One-O-One
I was a medic with a gun
Assigned to A Troop 2ⁿᵈ Squadron 17ᵗʰ Cav
I couldn't believe the adventure I was to have

Guard Engineers sweeping the road
Guard a convoy with an explosive load
Sweep a vill
Night ambush, looking for VC to kill

Securing a stretch of Highway One
Tuy Hoa to Tuy An. It was a job for the One-O-One
Air assault to a mountain top
Charlie movement comes to a stop

I lost friends in Vietnam
Proud to serve with each and every one
On my right shoulder, a Screaming Eagle patch
On my left, a Screaming Eagle to match

173ᴿᴰ Airborne Brigade

The 173rd Airborne was sent to Vietnam
Professionals to old Charlie Cong
Sky soldiers of 173rd
They preferred to call themselves, "The Herd"

They were committed to the Vietnam War
Combat troops who were followed by more
The 173rd Airborne added to its fame
Fighting in places they couldn't name

Combat jump into War Zone C
Assigned to the 173rd Airborne Infantry
The bloody battle at Dak To
They fought the NVA, a determined foe

They knew their job and did it well
Who knows how many Charlies, they sent to Hell
A winged sword on a field of blue
An Airborne tab for the chosen few

REALITY OF WAR

Death, destruction, pain and tears
War is not a game
You can't kill someone
Then have them get up

For dead is dead
Children die or get maimed for life
If you hurt a child, scar them forever
To say "I'm sorry" doesn't relieve the pain

Think of a friend, think of how it would be
To hold him as his blood soaks your clothes
Watch him as he breathes one last time
How do you tell his family they lost their
Son, brother, husband or father

War is not glory for those who die
Nor for those who lose a limb or sight
For after war, society will shun them
An embarrassment to be ignored
Veterans made to feel shame
Fighting a war, they didn't start

A Reason

Most GIs had someone special back home
A wife, a girlfriend, someone to dream about
Someone to drive away the fear
The fear of dying in this place called Vietnam

Sometimes she wouldn't wait
A Dear John would come from home
Depression would cause a man to lose his edge
An unseen movement, a sloppy step
An AK fires, maybe a booby trap

Was it suicide to ease a broken heart
Did his death cause a lost love any pain
No one can really say
The sadness was others were lost that day

Didn't the women understand
We had to have a reason waiting back home
A reason to survive one whole year
For a man to lose that edge
He would welcome death

FIRE SUPPORT

The 105 stood alone, its barrel pointing to the sky
The Grunts were in contact, from the radio the battle poured
Men sat on sandbags or lay upon the ground
Waiting for the call, they knew would come
The radio crackled, "Fire Mission"

They jumped and ran for their gun
With grim determination, they aimed the gun up North
They knew a wasted moment would could cost a G I life
In less than a heartbeat, the first round went out
An excited voice on the radio, "On target. Fire for effect!"

The men fired with a rhythm, a sight to behold
Sweat poured off sunburnt backs, gunsmoke filled the air
Tired and weary, they kept the tempo up
The radio blared, "Cease fire" It was music to their ears

The ambush had been broken, the VC were pulling back
They lay where they fell, exhausted to the bone
Days later, a message from the Grunts
All it said was, "Thank you, job well done"

FIRE SUPPORT BASE

Dawn greeted the morning, sunlight filled the air
The Firebase was silent, not a body moved around
The sound of approaching 'choppers broke the silence
Cobra gunships, Huey gunships, armed to the teeth
Zigging, zagging, passing each other up
Eager to make contact, be the first to draw VC blood
Their mission was to cover the Grunts coming up behind
Reinforcements, too late to save the Firebase

The 105 Howitzer's barrel pointed straight
A trace of smoke curled out the still warm end
The barrel like a finger pointing the way the VC came
A grim reminder of last night's ground attack
The VC attacked, human wave after human wave
Bodies stacked in piles. How many died it mattered not
Their mission was to destroy this G I camp

The Grunts searched the camp from end to end
Looking for wounded, someone who might have survived
All they found were the dead, silent for all time
Unable to tell them what happened last night
They found the loader who died loading one last round

The gunner died at his station, the cord gripped in his hand
Others died, locked in death with the enemy
Death scenes repeated time and time again
The Grunts knew they wouldn't forget this Firebase
It would be etched in their hearts forever

LESSONS NOT LEARNED

Up the trail, the Pointman went
Behind him, the Company followed
In our eyes, it was plain to see
The path was not the place to be

"Push on", the Captain said
"One more klick, stay on the path"
For those of us with time in Nam
To use a path was certain death

The explosion surprised us when it came
In the blast, the Pointman gone from sight
The firefight lasted into the night
The Captain called for flares to give us light
Green and red tracers lit the night
Colored fireflies darting out of sight

The noise was shattered by the sudden dead calm
In the dark, the VC slipped away
"Where's the Captain?" someone asked
Another voice joined in, "The Pointman's dead"
The Captain's voice boomed out, "Gather the wounded
Pull on back. Call for a Medevac"

Soon but not soon enough, the sound of 'choppers coming near
Into a clearing, the Medevac sat down
The Red Cross reflecting in the moonlight
An Angel of mercy, a sign of hope to save a life
And yet, not soon enough for my friend

Jungle Darkness

The jungle is a dark foreboding place
Feel the sun as it shines upon your face
Soon the canopy turns day into darkest night
It's only noon but no longer light

In the darkness, Charlie hides
You're ever watchful to the sides
You walk as quiet as a cat
You never know where Charlie's at

Sweat trickles down your face
Is it fear or the heat from this place
Jungle vines slow you down
Step over roots that protrude from the ground

The patrol takes a ten minute break
You eat C-rats, you learn to hate
The patrol is over as you head into clear blue sky
No contact but you're not sorry and that's no lie

BOOBY TRAPS

We swept the vill, not a VC to be found
Yet we lost men that day
We lost them to booby traps
Booby traps were an unknown fear

You can fight back an ambush or ground attack
But only a keen eye could detect the hidden booby trap
Miss the fishing line or jungle vine
Death was just a step away

For some, a fast death is preferred
To life without a limb or sight
Some adjust but others would rather die
Then be a burden to those they love

A Vietnam Christmas

I spent Christmas in Vietnam, one year
Odd place to celebrate Christmas cheer
On patrol, a Christmas wreath we found
A Chicom claymore exploded by the Viet Cong

We had green and red lights, late at night
Machine gun tracers blinking out of sight
Above our heads, stars gave us light
Parachutes flares illuminated the firefight

Santa's sled is coming in hot and fast
Charlie's present is dropped as he goes past
The 500 pound bomb will open itself
It's brand new right off the shelf

Heavy footed reindeer coming near
Reinforcements fighting Charlie to our rear
There will be no Christmas songs for us to hear
It's Gunships that will give us something to cheer

This was Christmas in the Vietnam War
Excitement, adventure, depression and more
I came home after I finished my year
To celebrate a different kind of Christmas cheer

THE MEDEVAC

Medevac in the sky, the jungle a heavy green
Thick, thick jungle, no one could be seen
Medevac pilot called for smoke
"Goofy grape" caused me to choke

The Medevac came in hot and fast
VC tracers arching past
I couldn't help but stare
How did the 'chopper stay in the air

Wounded and dead pushed inside
No time for a last goodbye, no time to cry
A wave to the pilot, he was ready to go
I thought he pulled out moving too slow

The pilot called back, he was taking fire
He gave it more power struggling to get higher
I remember the Red Cross on the door
Wounded and dead piled on the floor

My friends were leaving Vietnam
Thanks to one hellofa brave man
The Medevac Pilot was a hero to the G I
He helped some to live that might have died

They Didn't Care

Mail call came and went, no word from home
No one said, "Goodbye" when I left
No one said, "Take care of yourself
We'll miss you or we love you"
Maybe.....They didn't care

The war would be easier to take
If the family would, for heaven's sake
Breakdown and send me a letter
They don't know or understand
Why I had to come back to this war torn land
They make me feel as if.....They didn't care

Would it be so hard for them to write
Turn off the TV, lower the radio
Tell their family, "I have to write my lil brother"
I guess it's too much to ask. In time, the hurt will pass
It's just that they make me feel as if....They didn't care

"But you didn't write," They might say
"I was busy trying to stay alive." would be my reply
The worlds are so far apart
At home, they worry about what the family eats at night
Here, you cry as you look upon a body bag
It contains a friend who was like a brother

At home, they watch TV while I go out to ambush VC
They worry when their kids fall and get a scratch
We hit a hot LZ, I wonder will it be my last
Bullets crack overhead, grenades explode all around
Fragments fall as metallic raindrops in a storm
A friend is hit. I hold him as he dies
I can't cry anymore. Death is so common

I lie in rice paddy water and mud before we ambush VC
I look to the clear night sky and wonder...do they care
On the day, I go home. We'll be a family again
I'll hide the pain of knowing....They didn't care

Vietnam Heartbreak

I went to Nam, it was my choice
Complaint or gripe, I cannot voice

The Rain, the Sun bother me none
I remember you and the fun

The day I left and how you cried
"I love you, I will wait" you sighed

Six months went by and brought your last letter
"I cannot wait I found another"

But what of me, you ripped my heart
My eyes are heavy, the teardrops start

You were my world, you were my life
All I wanted was you….to be my wife

If home I stayed, you'd still be mine
We'd be together, life would be fine

Here I live in mud and sweat
No longer able to call you pet

In a year, I'll come home
Standing tall, no more to roam

I'll look you up to say hello
Then turn my back saying
"I have to go"

THE BATTLE

The Battle is over, the enemy gone
Can't be sure but I think we won
It's difficult to tell with so many dead
Hard to see through the dressing on my head

It was a fierce fight, as fierce as could be
They weren't VC but hardcore NVA Infantry
We fought and soon it was hand to hand
I couldn't see dying for some worthless land

Artillery shells exploding so near
I had to fight back, a thing called fear
I was scared I'll admit that fact
Thought of home, prayed to make it back

The wounded were pulled back to the rear
Some would be back to finish their year
Reinforcements mentioned our thousand yard stare
We made it out alive, we didn't care

THE POW

He's there, I know he is
I feel it deep in my heart
He's waiting, hoping and praying
For the day, he's set free
He went and fought for his country
We're right, thought he, to stop a commie plague

Captured, he was tortured for being a G I
He kneels in a bamboo cage
Too small to stand or lie down
His guards laugh and tease
Where's your country and your flag
Your country has turned its back
They say you don't exist

All he has left is trust in his God
A tear falls on his flag made from gathered rags
Why do politicians cast him aside
He fought their war, they didn't want to win
They're ashamed to admit…
They left him for dead

You Left Me

I sit in deep dark hole
Day to day survival, my only goal
Once I was a part of a team
Now I'm abandon or so it seems

Years come and then they're gone
My captors brag of the war they've won
I hold my voice I have nothing to say
Anything said would increase the torture each day

If the war is over, why am I still here
Abandon by my country, my biggest fear
I was loyal to my flag and country
There is no freedom bird waiting for me

Politicians refused to admit we're still here
They close their eyes, they don't want to hear
A few of us are waiting to this day
To the politicians, we just want to say

.......why did you leave me

D J Salute

His name it doesn't matter
We called him D J for his chatter
In the jungle, our patrol was hit
I dropped my ruck, grabbed my aid kit

The cry of "Medic", I jumped and ran
I was pushed by an unseen hand
D J took a round meant for me
I worked on him, thinking this cannot be

Dressing on dressing, the blood flowed free
His hand reached out and took a hold of me
In a whispered voice, he said goodbye
Before I knew it, I began to cry

The fight was over, the VC slayed
I covered his face and prayed
"Dear God, take him home, treat him well
He's already spent his time in Hell"

THE PREACHERMAN

He came to our platoon, a Bible in his hand
Tried to get us to change our ways
Said the day of redemption was at hand
Day after day, he saw his friends die
Soon he began to question why
Why his Lord allowed this to go on

Soon he left his Bible in his pack
He drank, he smoked and gambled with the rest of us
One day, he cursed. He cursed politicians
They started a war, we weren't allowed to win
And yet, he cursed himself for being so weak

In an open field, he fell to his knees
He begged forgiveness for going astray
A sniper found him that day, a shot rang out
Was he forgiven in that final moment
I can't say but as I placed him in a body bag
I made sure his Bible was in his hands

THE F N G

He came to the platoon, scared as can be
We took a long look at the F N G
We teased him but only in fun
Everyone started their tour with day one

We'd teach him to keep looking around
Claymores in tree tops, booby traps on the ground
How to spot the hidden pungi pit
Protect the Bandaid when someone was hit

He'd trigger an ambush like he was taught
Learn to kill without a second thought
Chopper assault into a hot LZ
He'd hear an AK cracking like an angry bee

He'd know the pain of seeing a friend die
When it's okay to be macho, when it's okay to cry
No longer the F'N new guy, he'd be a pro
He'd be accepted, he'd be a bro

THE KID

He was a kid who belonged back home
Telling his dad about the big game coming up
Maybe, a date with his favorite girl
His thoughts should have been
The prom, a job, a zit on his face

Now, he has no thoughts
An explosion took them away
I took one last look as I zipped him up
My eyes watered as I recalled
He came to me, "Doc, I have a rash"
He was embarrassed when I said it was only jungle rot

I took to him as if he were my kid brother
Standing up, I knew I lost a part of me
My heart was heavy as they took him away
I prayed his family would understand
All he wanted was to make them proud

A Test Of Faith

Deep in thoughtful prayer, the priest heard HIS call
"Go now to the war torn Asian land
Attend my flock. Let them know I still care"
Time flew before he stepped foot in Vietnam

He had his choice of where to go
He replied, "Where the fighting men need me most"
The 'chopper flew him to the jungle where he joined a patrol
He marveled at the beauty of a hidden valley
"God's work", he told a nervous grunt
The beauty shattered by sudden gunfire

He watched a young medic run to a wounded G I
The medic fell wounded, soon a lifeless form
He clutched the cross around his neck, one short prayer
"Lord, if this be your will, let me not falter"

He pulled a wounded G I to cover, sheltered a body with his own
In time, he felt his body ripped apart
As he died with one last gasp, "Lord, have mercy"
They found him where he fell and they knew
He'd gone home to be with his God

FRIENDSHIP

He looked too young, too young to shave
But in combat, showed he was brave
He liked to joke, have some fun
In the squad, he carried the heavy gun

In a fight, showed he was tough
With the "sixty", he knew his stuff
Talked of home, his girl, mom and dad
When he went home, they'd be so glad

After mail call, he came by
"I need to talk. You should hear
My girl left me, couldn't wait a year"
His young face showed such pain
I knew he'd never be the same

What to say....nothing there
Back home, she didn't care
She ripped his heart, it wasn't fair
He walked away, tears coming down
Sat and cried, how I wish she had lied

One day, it happened when we got hit
He fired from the open, gave me a fit
The AK hit him in the chest
He laughed and hollered, was that their best

He fired up his last belt
But the pain he must have felt
The VC hit him again and again
And I knew I lost my best friend

The fight was over, I picked him up
Called the medic who shook his head
"The VC killed him" the Lieutenant said
But I knew better.
She did....in her last letter

Final Farewell

The formation was called at sunrise
It was to honor four of the guys
They died in a firefight
An ambush gone wrong last night

In front of us, four rifles turned upside down
Topped by helmets, boots on the ground
Four sets to represent our friends now dead
From the Bible, the Chaplain read
"Dear Lord, bless these men. Let their souls be free"
Words couldn't describe the pain inside of me
They were my friends, now they're gone
Killed by the Viet Cong

With a final salute, we grabbed our gear
The VC would know our anger, the meaning of fear
In Vietnam, everyone paid the price
Life or death was a roll of the dice

THE CONSCIENTIOUS OBJECTOR

His name I don't recall
But I remember him as if it were yesterday
I asked why he didn't carry a gun
"I'm a medic", he said with a smile
Holding up my aid kit, I said "So am I
But I'll fight until I hear the call"

He smiled and explained to me
"My religion says it's wrong to kill
So I work to save another
I do my part so a G I can make it home"
He was harassed for refusing a gun
He'd smile and say, "It's not my way"

Later, I heard he lost his life
A firefight that grew more intense as it went on
The platoon watched, respect growing for this man
Who refused to carry a gun or take a life
He crawled amid bullets singing death
He worked in silence to save a life
Determination froze a smile on his face

His platoon praised him, too late for him to hear
He died for his beliefs
Others will follow him to carry a gun or not
For the medic was the unsung hero of Vietnam
The war, politicians refused to win

THE RTO

The RTO was the man of the day
Respect for him went a long way
Prime target for a VC gun
Being in someone's sights couldn't be much fun

Radio antenna sticking over his head
In a 'bush, he was as good as dead
The VC knew this man was the key
To kill him ensured their victory

Overhead, rounds cracking past
We need help and we need it fast
RTO's voice steady and calm
Asked the flyboys to drop napalm

He was good with his RTO talk
"Pappa Lima, this is White Chalk"
He called for Arty to give us a show
Gunships caught Charlie moving too slow

He called for a Medevac
To fly the wounded back
From the VC, he knew what to expect
Risking his life earned our respect

THE RAIDER

He wrote home to Mom and Dad
He was doing well, of that they'd be glad
Shipped to Nam, combat was something he didn't crave
But he wanted them to think of him as brave

He made up stories, told them lies
How he was a bro, one of the guys
A buddy wounded tripping booby trap wire
He saved his friend by running through AK fire

Of the VC charging in a human wave attack
Grabbing a "sixty", he fought them back
Helped a medic save a friend
The body count after the fight came to an end

We read his pilfered letter and we knew better
He never saw any of the combat that he wrote
For he was........

THE REMINGTON RAIDER

OUR FRIENDS

The Vietnamese are our friends
The President said
I looked at the body bag and thought
Sure they are, my friend is dead

"Our friends" watched as we went by
We could see hatred in each and every eye
Nothing was said of the VC lying in wait
We lost Phil. The VC lost eight

It didn't matter how many VC we kill
It wouldn't bring back my friend Phil
"Our friends" watched us walk back
A laughing wisecrack, an unconcealed grin
"Our friends" were loyal to Ho Chi Minh

From the VC, we knew what to expect
For "Our friends" we had no respect
A Medevac came to take Phil home
We wanted to burn the vill as Nero did Rome
America sent her young men to fight
When did the friendship end
And the hate begin

AID STATION DUTY

I walked through the Aid Station door
My combat dressings were gone I needed more
My fatigues were covered with blood and sweat
Morphine syrettes, something else I had to get

I put my ruck out of the way
Talked to the Head Doc who made my day
I had been wounded twice by Old Charlie Cong
He made a decision, it didn't take long

I was pulled from my line company
Aid Station duty was assigned to me
I felt bad leaving the guys in the Infantry
They were a family, they meant a lot to me

The guys wished me well
As they left on a mission, I felt like hell
I was now a REMF assigned to the rear
But now I'd make it home after my year

BROS

The patrol stopped for lunch
I looked at the patrol, a mixed bunch
Some volunteered for Nam, others were sent
We served our country, we knew what it meant

Johnson may have been black
But in a firefight, he protected our back
He joined to give his family a better life
All he wanted to do was go home to his wife

The El Tee was our leader, his skin was white
In contact, he was at the front of the fight
He wouldn't risk the life of one of his men
He gave the orders, we trusted him

Rico was pointman, his skin was brown
Going up a trail, he'd be checking around
He knew the patrol depended on him
If he missed any sign, our chances were slim

The color of our skins mattered not
We still cried when one of us was shot
Our blood was the same shade of red
They were my bros, no more need be said

THE RED CROSS GIRL

I walked through the Aid Station door
When I saw her, I let my ruck fall to the floor
A Red Cross worker was looking at me
An American woman, how could this be

A beautiful round eyed woman in a firebase
What did she think of this GI with a dirty face
My ruck and I were brown with Vietnam mud
I had been thinking of the EM club, drinking suds

She smiled and held out her hand
I nearly forgot I was in Vietnam
She reminded me of the girl next door
I forgot about living in the land of blood and gore

You can have the girls of this Asian land
I wanted an American beauty to walk with, hand in hand
Her smile reminded me of why I wanted to make it back
American girls had something Asian girls lack

I had no chance to thank this girl
She came a long way to make a GI's day
I still remember her after all this time
I use to dream, I'd make her mine

The Flight Attendant

She watched as they walked down the aisle
She welcomed them with a ready made smile
They talked with her, called her round eyes
They were typical American guys

GI's laughing, sharing a joke
A slap on the shoulder, a friendly poke
She heard pride in the way they bragged
Firing a sixty, tossing a frag

When they returned from five days of fun
There would be no laughter, their R&R done
It would be a quick trip back to the Vietnam War
They would be thinking of killing, dying and more

She felt her heart ache for every GI
Who would live, who would die
She hid her feelings, she wouldn't cry
All she could give was a smile to remember her by

VIETNAM NURSE

She walks the ward late at night
A mother hen watching over those she calls her own
She stops to check an unmoving form
A GI who has taken his last breath
Tears flow down her cheeks as she covers his face
Holds his hand, one more time
She looks to Heaven and asks God, "Why?"
Why one so young had to die

The day she came to Vietnam, such a long time ago
She vowed to herself, pain and suffering would bother her none
A cold heart to the cries of the wounded
A frozen face to those she knew would die
Without her knowledge, she knew not when
Her heart melted to these brave young men
Wounded who came on litter or in the arms of friends

Working, praying and sometimes a curse
She worked so hard to save so many
But yet, it was the ones she couldn't save
For these, she sought a private place
So others wouldn't see the tears she couldn't stop
In Vietnam, the nurse was many things
But to the wounded, she was a touch of home

Why Him?

Here's to a friend that survived his year
He went through a lot but showed no fear
Heavy contact with NVA in Tet of '68
To die in Nam was not his fate

A Buck Sergeant, in charge of the guys
He did his job, paid no attention to lifer lies
They promised him rank for a job well done
All he wanted to do was go home and have some fun

He survived Tu Dia Vill and its booby traps
VC ambush, firing rock and roll, busting caps
He was our leader but still one of us
When Lifers messed with us, how he would cuss

We were happy for him when he went away
He was happy at home, until one sad day
A friend wrote to let us know
He went swimming and drowned in the undertow

We heard the news and comforted each other
His death was hard on us for he was a brother
He survived Vietnam to go home and die
It didn't make sense. We asked, why him

WHY???

CIB/CMB

I watched a trooper walking by
My eyes focused on his chest
Medals amid ribbons showed he was a Vet

I gazed at his CIB, a rifle in a field a blue
It announced to those who never served
In Vietnam, he had been Combat Infantry

He looked toward my chest
My CMB was standing out
A Combat Medic, a Combat Grunt

Medals to attest our courage in Vietnam
To wear one of these fills one with pride
We took a walk that others feared

THE PURPLE HEART

I went to Nam to do my part
I didn't expect to earn the Purple Heart
I didn't know I'd been hit by flying lead
Until I felt blood running down the side of my head

It shook me up I could be dead
A fraction more would have blown my head
I felt no pain as the blood flowed free
I couldn't believe what happened to me

I didn't have time to think or swear
The fact I was hit gave me a scare
A dressing soaked up the blood and stopped its flow
Now all I have is a small scar to show

I'm proud of the medal I had won
I thought I'd be killed earning one
So many others earned the Purple Heart
But from their lives they had to part

THE STAR

I was given a Star
For fighting in a land far away
A Star for doing good
Doing a job, I knew I should

The ambush from a friendly vill
The Brass refused Arty from the hill
Bullets crack, they pop and sometimes zing
The damage they do to a human being

A dressing soaked in rice paddy mud
Turning red with my bro's blood
Infection can be treated in the rear
The loss of life is what I fear

I risked my life for my friends
If it's my time, this is the way it ends
I accepted the Star, I thought it right
It honors my bros that died in the fight

HOMEWARD BOUND

She sat pretty as could be
I knew she was waiting for me
She was my dream, she was my hope
I felt a small lump start in my throat

I never thought I'd see the day
She'd be here to take me away
She had many names, on one we agreed
Freedom bird sounded good to me

So many guys standing around
We knew soon, we'd be homeward bound
At a given time, we boarded the plane
The chaos was wonderful, slightly insane

We thought of friends, we left behind
The togetherness we shared came to mind
I grew up and aged in Vietnam
I arrived a boy and leave a man

As we became airborne, we cheered to a man
We were leaving a death called Vietnam
At the window, I watched the coast disappear
We all made a gesture, the meaning was clear

MY RETURN

I served my year and made it home
Thought it over, no more would I roam
But it wasn't meant to be
Vietnam was an itch deep inside of me

Vietnam was in the papers and on TV
It seemed to call and beckon me
I was safe at home, it didn't seem right
I had to go back, rejoin the fight

I put it off, day after day
Then told my sister I was going away
I was a medic. I belonged with the Infantry

I signed the papers sending me back
Part of me happy, part of me sad
I knew I might end up in a body bag
My grave marked only by an American Flag

Part of me didn't care
I had to return, my bros were there
Someone had to help them come home
I wanted them to know they weren't alone

THE VISIT

I remember the day, so long ago
My Father answered a knock on the door
An Army Captain and the local Priest
In the living room, they told Mom and Dad
My brother had been killed in Vietnam

Mom denied what they said
"My boy's okay, he'll be home soon", then she cried
With tears in his eyes, Dad asked how he died
"An ambush," the Captain said. "He felt no pain"

I walked away, blinded by my tears
I made my pledge to seek revenge
I'm old enough, I'll join up
When I get to Vietnam, I'll kill those who caused his death

Later Dad found me. Between my sobs, I cursed the war
The politicians who sent my brother to die
I put my face in my hands and cried
But so many others shared the same heart breaking pain

I CAME HOME

I came home from Vietnam, yesterday
The family was there to say hello
Momma cried but Dad held his back
My brother and cousins placed me in the car
I tried to reach out and hug my mamma
To wipe away her tears, to make her smile again

I came home from Vietnam, yesterday
Or at least my body did
I remember the ambush and a short lived pain
Somehow I found myself at home
To see the Army tell Mom and Dad
How I died in Vietnam

I wanted to holler or shout
To let them know not to cry over me
I did my duty, of that I'm proud
And I'm sorry to cause them such pain

I came home from Vietnam, yesterday
But no longer able to say, "I love you Mom and Dad"
I wanted them to know I feel no pain and I'm whole again
I have to go, a light beckons me

I see Grandpa, he died before I left home
He's smiling and holding out his hand
Says he's here to take me from this troubled land
I know I have to go but I'd like one more time
...........to hug my Mom and Dad

HONOR GUARD

It was an overcast day
Seven men stood far from the grave
Seven Veterans of the Vietnam War
They came to honor one of their own

They watched the family gather
Soon, six more Vets walking step by step
They carried the casket of a young man
A young man that died in the unpopular war

The Vets listened to the family cry
Parents, relatives and friends couldn't understand why
Why this special person had to die
Soon, even a Vet wiped moisture from his eye

The Priest asked his God to bless this man
Take him to Heaven, away from this troubled land
Seven Vets responded to a soft command
Seven rifles fired; once, twice, three times
Twenty-one guns to salute the fallen hero

As quiet settled over the crowd
They thought they were cried out
Off in the distance, a low mournful sound
The bugler played taps, a final farewell
The crowd found tears they didn't know they had

Six men folded the American Flag
The only reminder of this sad day
The Flag to show he died for his country
His mother clutched it to her chest
As if to hold onto her son

The Military Cemetery

I stand in silence, head bowed low
I look at white crosses row after row
Young men who answered their country's call
Young men marching off to war
I hear the battle, I hear the guns roar

The country has honored their sacrifice
One special day to mourn the loss of life
Friends and relatives will shed their tears
A grateful nation will reflect on past fears

Young men who gave their best
Now at peace, in eternal rest
Moisture runs down my face
I feel no shame in this hallowed place
As I leave, I look back once more
A fitting tribute for those killed in war

A LETTER TO HEAVEN

Dear GOD in Heaven

I found out my friend Jerry died in Vietnam
It's not my right to ask
Did you have an Angel escort him to Heaven
He returned to Vietnam and died in sixty-nine
I pray you let him live in that special place
The place you have for those who died in war

He had nothing to do with starting the Vietnam War
He went to fight for his country and his flag
A West Point officer and gentleman was he
He never considered himself better than me
Respect, he earned taking care of his men

His death was something I thought would be
But it still came as a shock to me
I'll miss his smile and good humored way
To describe the pain inside of me is hard to say
If by chance, you see him walking by
Just tell him First Platoon Doc said hi
Maybe we'll get together some day
Renew a friendship that slipped away

HEAR ME!

Hear me, America
Hear what I have to say
Last night, I sat and cried
I found out my friend Jerry died
He died in Vietnam, a long time ago
But time doesn't soften the blow

You forgot him, me and all the rest
For too many years, we did our best
To figure out our pain and unrest
We came home on the Freedom Bird
No celebration, no parade, no comforting word

You turned your back on us
As if we did something wrong
We didn't start the damn war
We came home and no longer fit
"Baby Killer" you hollered as you spit

What good did it do to fight the Vietnam War
Then come home and fight some more
It doesn't matter anymore
I'm still proud I fought in the Vietnam War

THE VIETNAM WALL

I went to the Wall
Or at least I tried
I wanted to remember my friends
Tell them, one last goodbye

To open my heart
And tell them I'm sorry
So sorry they died
And I miss them deep inside

I stopped before I got to the Wall
I tried to move but my feet were like lead
So many names, so many dead
Grief overcame me, memories flooded my head

Maybe one day, I'll walk the Wall
Find my friends, touch their names
I hope they understand....right now, I can't
The pain is too much....I just can't

THE HEALING PLACE

I went to the Vietnam Wall to find a friend
He served his country to the fatal end
Now he's a cherished memory inside of me
It's still hard to accept what had to be

I looked at the people standing, staring
In their faces, the pain, the love, the caring
A soft cry as one finds a loved one
Fingers trace a father's name, maybe someone's son

It's said the Vietnam Wall is a healing place
As tears of grief run down my face
The pain and guilt I buried deep inside
Flowed free in sobs, I no longer hide

I searched the Vietnam Wall looking for my bro
Memories flash of the hard times of long ago
As I find his name, a peaceful feeling flows through me
As if my friend is saying, you're finally free

WAS GOD IN NAM?

Was God in Nam? It's hard to say
It's a question that's argued to this day
I say yes. It's hard to explain why
For one thing, I didn't die

Some died that should have lived
To society, they had much to give
Who can really say who should be around
While others are now buried in the ground

Those who believe will always wonder
Did HE make a mistake. Did HE blunder
Those who don't believe will always sneer
Point to the pleas of the dead, HE didn't hear

Sometimes it's hard to understand
Why my friends had to die in Vietnam
Whether or not you believe in a God above
It was still nice to come home to those you love

A Grieving Dad

You were so proud of your high school grad
He enlisted in the military, just like his dad
Said he wanted to protect his country
Make it a better place for you and me

He came home on leave, one day
Took you aside, there was something he had to say
You knew he was headed to fight in the Vietnam War
You felt pride, fear and so much more

Your son had grown up to be a man
But you didn't want to lose your son in Vietnam
With a sigh, you gave him a hug
He didn't see your heartstrings given a tug

He wrote, at least once a week
Between the lines, you learned to peek
You knew from the media, the fighting was bad
He kept his letters happy not wanting you sad

That was then, today is now
They said he died but didn't say how
You looked at the medal, they said he won
With tears, you cried, "Damn the medal, I want my son!"

Clutching his medal, you felt him near
An unseen movement wiped away a tear
You looked at his grave, accepted the change
Life without him would be strange

A Mother's Pain

A mother sat at her son's grave
Held her head up trying to be brave
He was her only son
She remembered his smile and freckled face
His eyes, so full of life
Now he's gone, taken from her forever

He surprised her by joining up
Then came that awful day
Said he had orders for Vietnam
She hid her fears, kissed him goodbye
Letter after letter, she sent her son
Letters filled with a mother's love

One day, a knock on the door
She saw an officer, a Chaplain by his crest
Her heart skipped a beat inside her chest
And she knew before he said a word
Her son was gone, killed in Vietnam

As she sat, a tear flowed from her eye
Before she knew it, she began to cry
His death left her alone
From her lips came a low soft moan
She gazed at the headstone that held his name
And she knew nothing would ever be the same

LITTLE MAN

The boy stood at his mother's side
He cried because she cried
But he didn't understand why
Someone told him the box held his Dad
Is that what made his mother so sad

He heard a whisper, be brave little man
Your Father died in Vietnam
It is said, he died saving a friend
His thoughts were of you at the end

Have courage, little man
Hold your head up high
Stop those tears......don't cry
I know it's hard.......please try

Be proud, little man
Your Father died for his country
He died to keep us free
Your Dad's in Heaven watching from a cloud
Grow up to be like him, make him proud

THE LITTLEST VICTIM

The little girl stood in the first row
Her pretty dress, she wanted to show
Hands picked her up and sat her back down
Her Uncle looked at her with a frown

Her Daddy was suppose to be there
When she asked, "Where's Daddy?" people would stare
Her mother told her, he had gone to Heaven
She whispered, "He didn't tell me goodbye when he went"

She watched a box sink into the ground
Then she knew, with a sob, she looked around
Her Daddy wouldn't be there anymore
No hugs, no kisses, no wrestling on the floor

Now tears flowed free as she looked at the grave
"Goodbye Daddy, I love you and I'll try to be brave"
She put her head in her mother's lap and cried
She didn't understand Vietnam where her Daddy died

A Father's Farewell

Dearest son, as you read this letter
I wish things could have turned out better
It's to let you know I died in Vietnam
Sometimes a man has to take a stand

I didn't want to leave your mom or you
But the country's call was answered by so few
When you see the American Flag go by
I hope you'll hold your head up high

I'll miss watching you grow into a man
I left before your life really began
There will be no fishing trips to take you on
No fatherly embrace, no telling people, "This is my son"

I carry a picture of you next to my heart
It's worn and bent, the edges are starting to part
"I love you, son" is what I'm trying to say
You are on my mind, each and every day

I hope you'll always be proud of me
This isn't the way I wanted our lives to be
It's hard to describe how I miss you so
Goodbye son, I love you but I have to go

Dear Dad

I remember the day, so long ago
When I told you I had orders for Vietnam
You said you knew sooner or later I would go
I didn't know when you accepted I was a man

You never gave me a hug or said I love you
But I knew because I loved you too
I wanted you to know you brought me up right
Maybe that's why I felt I had to join the fight

All I wanted was for you to be proud of me
Tell the others with pride, "He's fighting for his country"
I thought in the fighting I might end up dead
A casket would be my final bed

It wasn't meant to be
The Lord took you instead of me
It doesn't seem right even to this day
I only wanted to say......I miss you

A Friend's Family

Walking through a department store aisle
I nodded my head at a young woman who gave me a smile
As I continued to walk, I felt a tug and looked to see
The same woman looking at me

She pointed to the patches on my worn torn jungle shirt
"My Dad wore the Eagle patch" her eyes filled with hurt
She asked me to tell her something of Vietnam
It had been a long time since I thought about Nam

We sat at a table in the cafeteria deli
I told her my name. She said her name was Shelly
I talked about the war but left out the blood and gore
Of friends lost, of friends, I'd see no more

A strange thing happened when I talked about my best friend
How he died in my arms and how I cried
From my wallet, I pulled a faded picture to show
With a whisper in her voice, "That's my Father!"

She told me she wanted me to talk to her Mom
To tell her how the man she loved had died
That night, I tried to explain, to let her mom know
Her lost love died saving me

A MEDIC'S TORMENT

When I sleep, I hear their cry
I sigh, an anguished, mournful sigh
I dream of my friends from the past
How long will my nightmares last

The Vietnam Syndrome, people say
It's affecting me on this late day
I mourn my friends I won't see anymore
They died fighting the Vietnam War

I was the medic. They called me "Doc"
I fought to save the wounded
I worked on so many but some I lost
It's their voices I hear in my sleep

I see their faces I hear their cry
"Doc, I'm hit. Don't let me die"
No matter what I did, it wasn't enough
Was there something I didn't do

In my grief, I would blame them
Blame them for dying on me
In the end, I blame myself
They looked to me to save their lives
I failed them
Failing them......I failed myself

THE LONELY VET

I sat in a bar, next to a man
Looking at me, he asked, "You go to Nam?"
I nodded, "Yeah, I did my time"
He showed me AK scars the size of a dime

From his wounds, he survived
The one that bothered him was deep inside
The sadness in his face was clear to me
He felt betrayed by his family

He talked of losing his wife
To a friend while he fought for his life
Relatives who laughed and said he was wrong
They protested the war and for the Viet Cong

No one was left to tell him he did right
I reminded him how we never lost a fight
Politicians were to blame for starting the war
Then leaving us alone to face public scorn

We talked and brought out our pain
We fought in different places but death was the same
Now he sat taller than he did before
We became friends because of the Vietnam War

A Vet Friend

I looked at the man standing in front of me
He had served in Vietnam with the Marine Corp Infantry
I also served but with the Army Airborne
We both lost friends that we mourn

We talked of how it was all the same
Khe Sahn, Dak To, it didn't matter the name
To lose a friend, you felt depression and sad
It was worse if they had kids waiting for their dad

Different places, different ground
We both patrolled wherever Charlie could be found
Monsoon rain, Rice Paddy mud, Jungle green
The Vietnam terrain was truly mean

He was a Marine with Marine Corp pride
I was Airborne and standing tall
We're Vietnam Vets, a fact we won't hide
We're proud we answered our country's call

THE HOMELESS VET

I looked down a dark alley
Past trashcans and rats covered with fleas
I saw a ragged form trying to shuffle away
I hollered at him and asked him to stay

As we met, in his eyes I saw no fear
He stopped, just close enough to hear
Wanting to be friends, I shook his hand
He told me a story of life in a faraway land

Of fighting and dying, of friends now dead
Of nightmares of war, the pain in his head
He fought a war he didn't really understand
Now he lives off the refuse of this wealthy land

He suffered fighting for his country
He lost his job, his home and his family
Society had no use for him anymore
His value used up fighting the Vietnam War

THE DISABLED VET

At a roadside check, each man did his part
But they missed a bomb in a peasant's cart
All he remembers was the sudden pain
A pain so terrible, it nearly drove him insane

Medics saved him and sent him home
He had no family and preferred to be alone
Sometimes the anger would well up inside
Before he'd scream, he'd look for a place to hide
So others wouldn't know his pain

In his wheelchair, he'd gaze into the sky
For years, he asked, why me? Why?
What did I do to get sent to this place
As he felt his tears run down his face

His anger left him, a long time ago
For his loss, all he has is a medal to show
At times, he wished they had let him die
He returned to his room with a heartfelt sigh

VET FRIENDS

One pushes a wheelchair, missing legs below the knees
He could have been you, he could have been me
Another lives in darkness, blinded in a firefight
A legless man, another without sight

On each other, they've learned to depend
Circumstances have made them friends
Cast aside by society, each one losing hope
They encourage each other, they learn to cope

Their families no longer come around
Relatives tell friends, they died in Vietnam
They fought because their country was at war
Now, years later, their country has shut the door

Politicians slowly erode their benefits away
Watch what politicians do....not what they say
The Disabled Vets aren't ashamed they went to fight
They just want their country to do what is right

A Vet's Rage

We were sent to Vietnam

Why?

We fought a useless, senseless war

Why?

Politicians sent us to die

Why?

My friend died in my arms

Why?

58,000 men died in Vietnam

Why?

Politicians left our POWs to die

Why?

CAN SOMEONE JUST F'N TELL ME

WHY????

i ….just…. want…. to…. know

why

Ever Notice

Ever notice how people look at you
When you tell them you're a Vietnam Vet
If they didn't serve, they shy away
Nervous of what you might do or say

How do you tell them. How do you explain
You're proud you're a Vietnam Vet. You feel no shame
You fought a war politicians refused to win
They turned their backs on brave young men

You answered your country's call
Remember your sacrifice, remember it all
Today, you stand out in a crowd.
You're a Vietnam Vet. You've a right to be proud

Nam Vet

I came home, you had nothing to say
When I reached out, you turned away
My life changed when I was there
You didn't understand, you didn't care

My nightmares are filled with fear
Adjusting would be easier, if you were here
You left, said you were afraid of me
Paid no attention to my plea

Nightmares of Nam, loss of love. The pain is twice
Often, I wonder why God spared my life
As days go by, my life is an empty shell
Maybe I did die and this is my hell

One day, Heaven's light will shine on me
Then my soul will be pain free
As hard as I try
I know it won't happen until I die

Respect Me

Respect me…. that's all I ask
I fought America's wars in the past
Proudly, I shed my blood on many a day
My brothers died fighting for the U.S. of A

Respect me for who I am
I have my pride, I am a man
I have Indian, African and/or Spanish heritage
Don't put me in a stereotype cage

You treat me equal only in a war
After war, I'm equal no more
You say the right things to my face
Then discriminate against my race

One day, you might understand
Why we fought so hard for this land
Then equal, I will truly be
All I ask of you is to….. respect me

MY FLAG

The Flag goes up at break of dawn
Flapping in a gentle breeze
Some say, it's just a cloth
But they don't understand

To me, it's so much more
It's my flag. It's your flag
A symbol of our country
The freedom for which it stands
The men who died to keep us free

I went to war not long ago
Proud to serve beneath my Flag
I shed my blood for what was right
I claim a shred of the smallest thread

Some say I'm wrong and burn the Flag
The thought tears me up
Only another Vet can really understand
To see it fly in a gust of wind makes me proud
I did my duty, I served my time

A Painful Memory

I remember long ago
You chanted, "I won't go"
You didn't go but I went to fight
I still think what I did was right
You thought I was a fool
Called me a war monger's tool

You protested the war, started a riot
In Vietnam, we just couldn't buy it
You said the war was wrong, it shouldn't be
You burned the Flag that meant so much to me

You protested, said it was your right
Did you sleep better, knowing a GI died that night
We came home, you had a fit
GIs, you attacked, on our uniforms you spit
I'm proud I served, where I had been
Your protests to me were a sin

Years later, you have nothing to say
You won't say what you did that day
Now it's okay to say, "I served in Vietnam"
All you can whisper is… "I meant no harm"

VACATION

I went away to fight for my country
I came back with deep concealed pain
You pretended I was on vacation
Death, destruction, blood and guts
Does this sound as if I had fun

I killed people I didn't know
Men, women, the young and the old
I killed before they could kill my friends
I learned to kill in different ways

My hands, a knife, a booby trap
An M-16 on rock and roll
I brought down the heavens
Artillery, Gunships, Fighter planes
B-52s with their silent death

You pretended I went to sun filled beaches
Bikini clad females, surfers riding waves
Nightclubs, dancing 'til wee hours of night
Buying souvenirs to pass around

How could you know what I did to survive
You have yet to ask me how it was
It doesn't matter. I couldn't tell you
.......You had to be there

POLITICIANS

They said Vietnam should be free
To the Vietnam War, they sent you and me
Sending the Army and Marine Corps

Each in Congress had their say
There was no price too big to pay
A few said no but were voted down
The draft affected each and every town

But what of the GIs they sent to fight
Forgotten......for they were out of sight
They cared not for us that was clear
They worried more about their political career

Soon, too many GIs buried in the ground
Protests caused the politicians to turn around
"We didn't vote for it" was now the cry
Then tell me why.... we were sent to die

WRONGED

During the Vietnam War, the Media did us wrong
It felt as if they were for the Viet Cong
It was popular to put the military down
Cause the public to squirm and frown

They put us on page one, inflamed antiwar heat
Tried to show us as an Army in defeat
They showed pictures of our dead, day after day
Freedom of the press is our right, they'd say

They took our victories on the ground
Showed us losing by turning them around
They made us to be bad guys
Hiding behind their media lies

Their public attitude against the war
Indirectly caused us wounded, dead and more
The news encouraged the Viet Cong, that's a fact
Because of their slant, how many GIs didn't come back

I'D LIKE TO KNOW

No one can tell me why
In Vietnam, I didn't die
It's a question that bothers me
I have no wife or family

Others had so much more
They had everything to live for
And yet God took them away
More or less told me I had to stay

He let me live but didn't say why
Sometimes I'm so down I want to cry
I found others feel the same
In a small way, I feel shame
I lived but I will never be the same

Maybe one day, He will let me know
Give me a vision to show
Why I survived the Vietnam War

DON'T ASK

I went to Nam to do my part
My memories are buried deep in my heart
I don't brag, I don't crow
I know what I know

War stories, I have no need to tell
It's enough I went through Hell
Don't ask how many did I kill
Don't ask, how did I feel

It's my choice, the memories I recall
My healing on visiting the Vietnam Wall
All of us Vets share an unspoken pride
We remember our bros who survived and those who died

I'm a Vietnam Vet, that's all I have to say
My experiences changed me to this day
Each day, I enjoy life so much more
A lesson earned surviving the Vietnam War

GUILT

The young man sat down and cried
His family didn't understand why
If only they could look deep into his soul
It ached from the guilt and pain that tormented him
He came home from Vietnam, a shadow of his former self

As a kid, he liked to talk, always had friends around
Now he's quiet, too quiet at times
His friends quit coming by
Said something about his vacant stare
As if he saw something they couldn't see

They were right, you know
He stared into his past, back to Vietnam
He remembered his platoon and the ambush on one hot day
The cries of the wounded refused to let him be
The silence of the dead, a cry in its own

He sits and wonders why, why he didn't die
So many of his friends lost in a useless war
He feels he didn't deserve to live
He should be buried on hallowed ground
With his friends from Vietnam
For only they shared the pain of fighting a war
Politicians refused to win

Judge Not

Now that the man is gone, some people sneer
He's with his Lord so he can't hear
The uncaring laugh, for they don't understand
They didn't see what he saw in Vietnam

The years have passed but his memories remained
All this time, he concealed his heartbreaking pain
Nightmares and guilt were always by his side
Who knows how many nights....alone....he cried

Before you condemn this soft spoken man
Step into his shoes during his tour in Vietnam
Can you say death wouldn't bother you
It bothers me for I was there too

Maybe his choice was the wrong one
It wasn't an easy choice but peace has finally come
That heavy burden has been removed from his chest
Let him be.....Let him rest

THE DARKNESS WITHIN

I feel it now and then
It comes but I can't say when
Like a blanket, it covers my heart
To describe this feeling I cannot

Vietnam is the cause of my sorrow
The pain and guilt of long ago
Sealed into the deepest part of memory
It has escaped to remind me

The sudden death, I was witness to
The cries for help from friends I knew
Brave men died, too many died
While back home, loved ones cried

I'll accept the burden given me
My past, a part of the present me
I'll accept the grief, a small sacrifice
To honor my bros who lost their lives

WHY

People ask, "Why?"
Why I write of the sadness
Of death and dying in Vietnam
I write what I know best

Concealed emotions, I try to lay to rest
All of us who fought have that special hurt
We fought a war, two decades long
Returned home to our country's scorn
Vets, who had to hide where they had been

Panama, Grenada, the first Persian Gulf War
The country's celebration for short quick wars
Some of us feel we were cast aside
An afterthought, in the Victory parades
The President said, "You too, Vietnam Vets"
As he tried to heal our pain
How can he know how we really felt

Some are bitter, the lies we had to live
But the Vietnam Vets will be the first to extend a hand
To the Vets of the latest wars
To say to them, "Welcome home, you have joined the
brotherhood"
For only Vets can tell how it was to expect death
Each day and night

THE CATHOLE

On patrol, I'm soaked in sweat
Fresh water, I need to get
I'm hot and thirsty, my canteen is low
I drink green water that doesn't flow

Later on, in the day
My gut rumbles in an urgent way
An aching in my tush
Grab a shovel, headed for the bush

Dug a cathole latrine
Those VC microbes sure were mean
Returned to the patrol with a smile
Ready to hump one more mile

LATRINE BURNER

New in country, I didn't know squat
First Sergeant's mad at me, he was really hot
Told me to burn the Captain's latrine
I should have asked, what did he mean

I was told to pour diesel fuel in the can
Toss in burning paper, kick back and get a tan
Check the mess when the fire burned out
I thought I knew what they were talking about .

Filled the can to the top, went for matches in my tent
First Sergeant found me sleeping, got slightly bent
I was angry when I tossed burning paper in the back
An explosion and flames engulfed the shack

The Captain let out a horrifying scream
Even now, I can hear it when I dream
They changed my MOS to eleven B
Shipped me to the boonies to get rid of me

The guys in the squad laughed at my tale
Told me to be glad, I wasn't in Long Binh Jail
I said I thought the Captain acted like an ass
But that's where I burned him with high test gas

Don't Mean Nothin'

Joined the Army, had lots of time
Thought you'd serve in peacetime
Nam broke out, now you're stuck
DON'T MEAN NOTHIN'

Going to war
Going to die
All for Mom and apple pie
DON'T MEAN NOTHIN'

Ain't no time to cry
We're going to die
Don't ask me why
DON'T MEAN NOTHIN'

Have no fear
Charlie's near
Has all his combat gear
DON'T MEAN NOTHIN'

Walked into a 'bush
Walked into a trap
Walked into the killing zone
DON'T MEAN NOTHIN'

Your friend is dead
Shot through the head
He's in his final bed
DON'T MEAN NOTHIN'

If at home, you're in your bed
Wake up to find your dead
Remember what I said
DON'T MEAN NOTHIN'

Jump School

The plane was dancing to and fro
I wish the Jumpmaster would holler go
When I went Airborne, it was a fluke
Now I'm airsick, I need to puke
Jumpmaster leaning out the door
"DZ coming up! Stand in the door!"

Framed in the door, first man in the stick
Forgot my stomach, suddenly I'm not sick
Combat jump, plane pops up to 1200 hundred feet
Green light on, men disappear
I hit the door without any fear
No holler of Geronimo, just count to three
Propwash pushes me, I'm pulled by gravity

Sudden stop, I check and see a full canopy
I look around for miles and miles, damn this is neat
I hear a command beneath my feet
Treetop level, I prepare to hit
All I could think was, "Aww shit"
A backward fall, more like crash and burn
It wasn't the fall, they made me learn
I stand up, I'm in a stupor
Five jumps, I'm an AIRBORNE PARATROOPER

Airborne Pride

Hanky hopper, that's what he called me
I looked at him with a puzzled grin
Airborne, Paratrooper, he explained
Pointing to himself, World War Two
My chest swells with pride, One-O-One, Vietnam
He smiled and said, One -O -One, Eighty Deuce, the Herd
It doesn't matter, we're all the brotherhood

We talked of how it was
The Airborne shuffle, standing in the door
The wind like a demon trying to pull you out
The green light on. Jumpmaster hollering, " Go!"
The free fall, count to three
The opening shock of the canopy
Slip and slide, adjust your direction
Treetop level, prepare for the PLF
A quick thud, you're on your feet

I looked at him, a mist in his eyes
We talked and he remembered how it was
Age didn't matter to us
Two troopers bonded by Airborne pride

Other Sights

We talk of Nam and firefights
Nothing is mentioned of the other sights
Vietnam was an open zoo
Elephants, Tigers, Snakes and Monkeys too

Packs of Orangutans running free
We'd see them swinging from tree to tree
Water Buffalo that hated the smell of GI
Big f'n rats staring you eye to eye

Rice paddy leeches felt like a kick in the shin
Jungle leeches were small but covered your skin
Twelve inch scorpions, claw to stinger end
Uck you lizard, strange message that it sends

Pissant bites that could make you scream
Centipedes, millipedes were ugly and looking mean
Gnats and mosquitoes buzzing around your face
Damn, I was glad to leave that place

I Remember

: odor of burning diesel fuel, burning latrines

: waking up soaked in sweat

: friends who became my bros, bros who didn't make it

: sharing c-rats, care package from home

: packing a ruck, M-16 mags, M-60 ammo, frags, smoke grenades, claymores, aid kit

: that lonely feeling of no mail at mail call

: boonie payday, no place to spend $50

: sitting in a chopper door, legs dangling out

: dumping chlorine water for fresh mountain water

: clean fatigues after weeks in the boonies

: sleeping to artillery fire, monsoon showers

: filling sandbags, digging foxholes, bunker building

: search and destroy missions, ambush patrols, Hot LZs

: rice paddies, leeches, knee deep mud, neck deep water

: wop, wop of hueys, cobras, rockets firing, artillery bursts

: explosions, AK fire, M-16 fire, thumpers exploding, RPGs, Frags

: individuals, squads, platoons fighting, dying, hollering, screams of medic

: medics calling for dustoff, dustoffs coming and going

: wounded GIs, blood soaked fatigues, blood on my hands not mine

: Freedom bird lifting off

OTHER REFLECTIONS

CONTENTS

SHE'S ALONE

In the darkness, she cried
There was no one by her side
The darkness used to conceal her fears
Darkness in her life, part of her fears

She cried because no one special was there
All she wanted was someone special to hear
Someone to comfort her, someone near

I wanted to reach out, stroke her hair
To gently let her know I was there
I couldn't reach her, her wall was too high
I'd wait until she let her hurt go by

I'd give her a hug, a reassuring smile
To let her know happiness would take a while
We'd walk, we'd talk and in the end
I hoped she'd understand I was her friend

I'm Your Friend

I'm your friend, you are mine
If you need to talk, I have the time
When days are dark, the future grim
You feel alone, your hopes are dim
Remember me, I'm your friend

When your troubles seem to pin you down
You find your smile turned upside down
When memories come back to haunt
You look around, a friend you want
Remember me, I'm your friend

If at times, you're sad and blue
Talk to me, I'm there for you
On a shoulder, you need to cry
Give me a call or just come on by
Remember me, I'm your friend

The darkest day, the blackest night
Sometimes a hug is such delight
A smiling face, a singing bird
Keep in mind, my last word
Remember me, I'm your friend

Goodbye, My Friend

I heard she's leaving, someday soon
I asked why she's going away
"I need something better." She said with a smile
"Don't go. I'll miss you." I wanted to say

I'll miss the smile she'd give to me
When we talked, she made me feel carefree
I'll miss her beautiful face
Without her, this won't be the same place

I know I'm not going to see her anymore
My heart will break when she walks out the door
She'll say, "We'll keep touch. We're still friends."
But I know that soon our friendship will end

When she's gone, my heart will have an empty spot
I hope she understands her friendship meant a lot
But friends don't stand in each other's way
They wish them well and hope they meet again another day

DARKNESS

Darkness surrounds one
It chokes so you cannot breathe

In the Darkness, hide your fears
They know you, they scare you

They feed upon your fear
And grow by leaps and bounds

They come in dreams
You dare not sleep

Tuck the blanket under your chin
Let it not touch the ground
For there, Evil crawls

Pray for daylight soon to come
To chase away your fears

But remember, before it's too late
Nighttime will come again

I DON'T CRY

Some people look at me and wonder
They wonder why I don't cry
I lost my father, mother and brother
Yet not a tear left my eye

They don't understand, they think I'm cold
I don't cry because I don't think it's right
To bare your emotions for all to see

I've seen death, so much death
I learned to put the pain deep inside of me
To keep it locked until I feel its time
Then I'll let it go but only when I'm alone

No one will see how much pain is inside of me
Some say that's wrong but who are they
To say what's right for me

MY BROTHER

My brother has left the family
He's missed by my sisters and me
Maybe others don't care
But our loss doesn't seem fair

He never bothered anyone
He wanted to be left alone to have some fun
He was a quiet easy going guy
I have an emptiness deep inside

Once he said he admired me
It was a surprise to me. It came so free
I always looked up to my brother
He never considered me to be a bother

His absence still leaves me feeling sad
But I know he's okay, he's with my dad
Maybe the Angels decided he was their kind of guy
Every now and then, I still look to Heaven and ask

why

THE LIGHT

I want to leave
This thing called reality
Where I was before my birth
I was happy. It was peaceful

A Heavenly light shined all around
There was no pain, hurt or despair
No wars, no plague, no crime
I was told to come. It was my time

It was then I felt sadness
I said to the Light, I don't want to go
But it was not my choice
There was a reason for my new life

I still don't understand what it is
What I'm supposed to do with this new life
I'll bid my time
Then maybe I'll be allowed to return to the Light

I Like Dreaming

I like dreaming
For reality is left behind
I can fly like a bird
Soar until I touch the sky
Float like a snowflake to the ground

I like dreaming
For it's an escape from my life
I can leave everything behind
I can be whatever I want to be

I like dreaming
For in my dreams, you're mine
I can reach out and hold you tight
Dreaming a life that's right for me

I like dreaming
But soon, too soon, it's over
I wake to face my reality
Reality would still be okay
As long as your love belonged to me

MY DREAM

Eyes so fair
Hair a golden brown
Skin so soft and smooth
She's the one I'd live my life with
If only she would care

I look at her and see my heaven
She looks at me and sees me not
For her, I'm not there
Someone she met, dismissed without a second thought

I can dream
But dreams rarely come true
I can dream
For dreams are better than what I have

HAPPINESS LOST

My days were dark as night
I wandered aimlessly
No goal in life, no reason to be

You entered my life
You brought me sunshine and beauty
You made me laugh
You gave me hope

All I am, all I will be
I owe to you
I live to be with you
To touch, to hear, to hold

And now you're gone
Emptiness has returned
Why did you come into my life

You showed me happiness then took it away
I'll live as I had before
Darkness…. Despair…embrace my return

LOST LOVE

I saw her walk past my sight
Come back, I wished with all my might
Not often does one meet a dream
She returned and gave me a hug

Heaven meant for us to meet
I caress her, hug her tight
I inhale, she smells so fresh
Her hair is soft, shines on its own

I cup her face, tilt so I can see
Her eyes are deep dark pools
I swim, I drown, I can't let go
I kiss her lips, they taste so full

She pulls back, a tear flows down
She says no, it cannot be
Her father says I'm not for her
Her religion is not mine

I believe in God, as do you
What matters what church we say our prayers
One last hug, our hands slip apart
Her lips say I love you then she's gone

I feel shattered, my heart beats on
But only as a tool, why go on
Nothing will be the same

A Thoughtful Moment

I sit and wonder why
Why I live day to day

Like my dreams never met
My youth is gone I cannot fret

I live my twilight years
Being alone, one of my fears

As for my dreams, I'm losing hope
Reality is gone as a puff of smoke

Some day when I pass on
No one special to mourn my being gone

I feel cheated, I feel sad
I won't have the family I wanted so bad

I lived my life, what a glory
Now I'm old, decades past forty

If there's a better life where I go
Then I'm ready....death don't be slow

Tell my sisters not to mourn
I go alone as I was born

GOODBYE BROWNIE

There came a knocking at my door
It sent shivers to my very core
The Grim Reaper was waiting outside
He came for Brownie who wouldn't hide

I wouldn't answer, maybe he'd go away
But I knew Death wouldn't wait another day
Death entered, there was no doubt
It was colder inside than out

Brownie picked up his head and looked at me
As if to say, Death would set him free
He closed his eyes and then he died
I touched his face one more time and cried

I'll miss Brownie, as a friend he was the best
He's no longer in pain, he's at rest
I'm alone now…alone and sad
Brownie was the best dog I ever had

CHRISTMAS

Christmas is a very special day
It's not for Santa and presents as some say
Kids opening their presents, their screams and shouts
People forget what it's really all about

It's for what happened, a long time ago
A child was born wrapped in a special glow
He came to save us, you and me
Encourage us to keep our souls sin free

On the day, he was crucified and died
The Angels and the Faithful cried
He rose and went to heaven
Where He sits at his Father's side

So when you enjoy your Christmas dinner
Remember He died for you and me, each a sinner
Bow your head and pray to be forgiven
One day, you might join him in Heaven

WHITEMAN'S PEACE

The Indian Chief stood looking around
Death, destruction, teepees burnt to the ground
He thought, Whiteman's way, Whiteman's peace
His arm bleeding from a bullet crease
He told his warriors prepare for the warpath
Let the Whiteman feel Indian wrath

He had trusted a Whiteman with hair the color of snow
His people had to be safe but there was no place to go
The Whiteman was many, like pine needles on a tree
He didn't want war but his people must live free
They left camp at a hurried pace
A few Indians, the last of a proud race

The Whiteman wanted Indian ground
Greed for the gold metal he found
They forced Indians onto worthless land
Then refused the promised helping hand
Now some feel a belated shame
They didn't understand Indian pride
Nor from where it came

FAMILY DISTURBANCE

She sat on the couch, bruised black and blue
He sat next to her, his attitude calm and cool
She wiped a trickle of blood from her chin
He intimidated her so she wouldn't turn him in

She said everything's okay, she just fell
She was scared of him that I could tell
Later, he'd say he was sorry and she'd forgive
I couldn't understand the life she chose to live

If she'd press charges, we'd take him away
But she worried about paying bills day to day
Later they'd admit the truth about tonight
An argument that led to the fight

A fight that didn't take long
She the weaker, he the strong
A 911 call brought us to their home
They argued for us to leave them alone

These calls happened time after time
Didn't men understand, spouse abuse was a crime
I looked at her as if to say
I knew we'd be back another day

GANGS

The child lay upon the ground
Shell casing scattered around
He should be living, playing, having fun
Now he's dead, one hand clutching a gun

He joined a gang to prove he was a man
He'd protect the block that was his plan
The police had a list calling him hardcore
He became involved in a drug war

His homeboy was shot hanging around
He cried as his friend was put into the ground
Grabbing his gun, he went out the door
All he said was he'd even the score

Several boys in a car waited for him
Against semi-automatics, his chances were slim
Now his parents cry each and every night
They lost their son. It didn't seem right

PUSHERMAN

Pusherman, Pusherman
Hooking kids throughout the land
How many die, you don't care
As long as the money is there

Pusherman, Pusherman, how do you feel inside
Knowing kids are setting their lives aside
Paying you for their final ride
Do you laugh, thinking of the times you lied

Pusherman, Pusherman, is your heart filled glee
Knowing their parents will live in misery
Burying their kids who listened to you
Their only crime was having nothing to do

Pusherman, Pusherman, selling you death to go
Your master is proud of you in Hell below
One day, Pusherman, he will come for you
With other pushers, your soul will burn too

As Satan laughs, you will understand too late
You've done his bidding. You've earned your fate
Don't look to Heaven, don't start to pray
They don't want to hear what you have to say

The Abused Child

The little child lay upon the bed
Bruises from ankles to head
I wondered, how could this be
This child should be playing, laughing, happy as can be

Now he lies with tubes running in and out
I see his still form, I want to shout
Is there no justice for this little one
Who will no longer run nor have fun

To protect themselves, they say he fell
Dear God, send them to burn in Hell
For those that loved the little one
They knew where the bruises came from

Little child, hear these words from me
If it were in my power, I'd set you free
I'd like to see you standing in front of me
'til I picked you up and set you upon my knee

The joy has gone from your eyes
I wish you could hear their damn lies
I'd like to pick you up, hold you in my arms
I'd like to protect you from further harm

All I can do is to pray to God above
To give you what you deserve....
Lots and lots of love

GLOSSARY

AK- short for AK 47, rifle carried by Viet Cong and North Vietnamese Army

Arty- shortened form for Artillery

Bandaid- Nickname for medics used by Army for radio transmissions instead of Medic

Booby trap- hand grenade, artillery round or other explosive hidden, set to explode when a hidden trip wire is hit by a GI

Brass- referred to upper echelon of command structure

Bro- term given to those considered closer than family due to sharing dangers of Vietnam

Buck Sergeant- E-5, lowest of NCO ranks

'bush- ambush, surprise attack

Bush, Boonies- in the field, looking for the enemy

Busting caps- firing weapon

Cathole- improvised toilet using entrenching tool to dig small hole

Charlie- nickname given to Viet Cong, sometimes used for NVA

Chicom- Chinese Communist as in Chicom grenade

Chopper- nickname for helicopter due to chopping noise from rotor blades

CIB- Combat Infantry Badge

Claymore- Anti-personnel mine

CMB- Combat Medical Badge

CO- Conscientious Objector, one who refused to kill due to religion

Contact- combat with enemy

C-Rats—C-rations, food usually eaten in field

Dear John- letter sent by loved one breaking off relationship

Didi- slang for get out of here, scram, beat it

Doc/Head Doc- nickname given to medics, Head Doc was Battalion Surgeon

DZ- drop zone for paratroopers jumping from aircraft

Eighty-Deuce- nickname for 82nd Airborne Division

Firebase- semi-permanent field base for supporting troops in field

Fire mission- artillery firing in support of troops engaged in contact

Freedom Bird- civilian aircraft used to ferry troops out of Vietnam

Goofy Grape- purple smoke used to identify location to aircraft

Gunships- helicopters armed with machine guns or rocket pods

Hot LZ- landing zone for troops surrounded by concealed enemy troops

Human Wave- enemy attacking in large formations

Hump- walking, patrolling country side looking for enemy

Jungle Rot- infection, skin condition caused by damp environment

Killing Zone- area in ambush where everyone should be killed

Lifer- one who makes military a career

Lt- shorten for Lieutenant, also pronounced El Tee

Medevac- military helicopter used to evacuate wounded from battlefield

Napalm- jellied gasoline

One-O-One- 101st Airborne Division

PLF- parachute fall taught to avoid injury after jumping from aircraft

Pointman- first man in patrol looking for enemy, booby traps or enemy sign

Pungi pit- covered hole with sharpened bamboo stakes

Rear- relatively safe area where support troops lived

REMF- name given to those who stay in rear, rear echelon m...f...

Remington Raider- anyone in rear safe area that writes home of contact not experienced

Rock and Roll- firing weapons on full automatic

Round Eye- name given to any woman, usually Caucasian, for shape of eyes

Stand Down- several days spent in rear to rest, resupply and get reinforcements

Stick- line of paratroops in plane waiting to jump

The Herd- unofficial name given by paratroops in 173rd Airborne Brigade to themselves

Thousand yard stare- faraway look from witnessing too much contact or killing

Tu Dia- Vietnamese warning to villagers of booby trap near

Vietnam Syndrome- also called PTSD- post traumatic stress disorder

War Monger-name given by war protestors to those who fought in the Vietnam War